CAN YOU BELIEVE IT?

- THE WORLD OF MACHINES -

Written by
JENNY VAUGHAN
Illustrated by
SALLIE REASON

CHERRYTREE BOOKS

A Cherrytree Book

Designed and produced by Templar Publishing Company Ltd,
Pippbrook Mill, London Road, Dorking, Surrey RH4 1JE

First published in 1990
by Cherrytree Press Ltd,
a subsidiary of
The Chivers Company Ltd,
Windsor Bridge Road,
Bath, Avon BA2 3AX

British Library Cataloguing in Publication Data
Vaughan, Jenny *1947–*
The world of machines.
1. Machinery
I. Title II. Series
621.8

ISBN 0-7451-5079-9

Typeset by Southern Positives and Negatives (SPAN),
Lingfield, Surrey
Colour separations by Chris Willcock Reproductions,
Maidstone, Kent
Printed and bound by Proost N.V., Turnhout, Belgium

PICTURE CREDITS

Key: Top = t, bottom = b, left = l, right = r

Front cover: tl Mary Evans Picture Library; br Peugeot Talbot Motor Company Ltd.

Page 4 Tom McHugh/Science Photo Library; page 7 Graham Ewens/Science Photo Library; page 9 Peter Riley/South American Pictures; page 10 Birmingham International Airport plc; page 12 bl Mary Evans Picture Library, tr British Gas plc; page 15 IBM UK Ltd; page 17 Rover Group; page 18 tr Science Museum Library; page 18–19 Lafontant/French Railways; page 20 Ministry of Defence; page 23 Mary Evans Picture Library; page 24 Mary Evans Picture Library; page 25 NASA/Science Photo Library; page 26 br Focalpoint, Norwich (Lotus production line); page 26–27 Courtesy of British Airways; page 28 The National Motor Museum, Beaulieu; page 33 Jeremy Flack/Aviation Photographs International; page 35 Mary Evans Picture Library.

CONTENTS

? ? ? ? ? ? ? ?

1. Is a nutcracker a machine?

A nutcracker is a machine and so are many simple things that we use every day. A machine is anything that helps to make a job easier to do. A nutcracker makes it possible for someone to break the shell of a nut, even though they would not be strong enough to do it with their hands. Most nutcrackers are made of a pair of ***levers*** *(see page 6). A lever is a bar, which we use for lifting or moving something. A see-saw is a lever – so that means it is a machine too.*

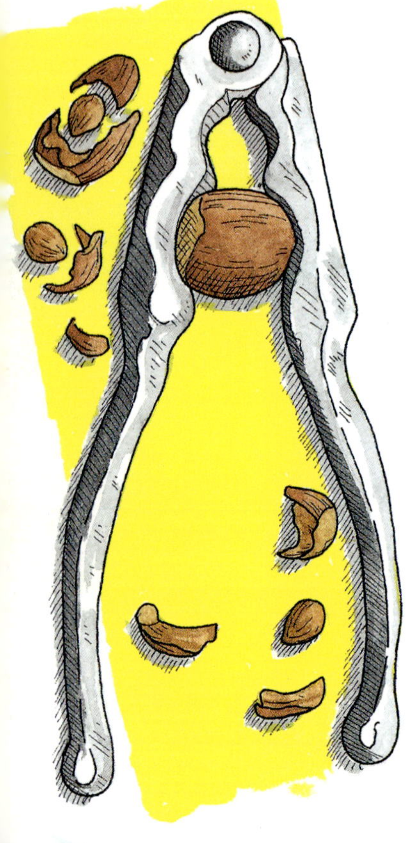

2. Can we get electricity from the wind?

We can use the power of the wind to make electricity by using a special kind of ***windmill****. A windmill has large sails, that turn in the wind. This action can be used to power machinery. In the past, this might have been used in a flour mill to grind corn, or to pump water, but some modern windmills, like the ones below, work generators to make electricity. A windmill like this will only work in very windy areas, where the average wind speed is about 32 kilometres an hour (kph). This only happens on remote islands or other places where strong winds blow in from the sea.*

Another way to make electricity from the wind is by using the power from waves in the sea. The wind makes the waves, and the movement of the waves is used to work a generator.

3. Did people actually think the Titanic was unsinkable?

The Titanic *was a luxury liner that sank on its first voyage in 1912. Its hull (body) was divided into 16 watertight compartments. Even if four of these compartments were flooded the ship would still float. Everybody thought that it was unsinkable. But when an iceberg struck the ship at 2.20 a.m. on April 15th, five of the compartments filled with water and the ship sank. More than 1,500 people were drowned. In 1985 the wreck of the Titanic was found lying on the ocean floor at a depth of about 3,950 metres.*

4. Were helicopters really invented in the Middle Ages?

The first helicopter was made in 1907. But there was an idea for one much earlier. Leonardo da Vinci was an Italian inventor, sculptor and artist who lived between 1452 and 1519. He made drawings of many inventions, including flying machines. In about 1483, he designed a machine that, if it had been built, would have flown like a helicopter.

5. Was there once a law that said no one could drive a car faster than 4 miles (6.5 kilometres) an hour?

The first cars were steam-driven stage-coaches. They could go at about 30 mph (48 kph) but could not stop easily. In 1865, a law was passed to stop them going faster than 4 mph (6.5 kph) and even slower in towns. Someone had to walk ahead with a red flag to warn people that the coach was coming.

6. Can a ship sail against the wind?

Sailing ships travel by being blown along by the wind – so you might think that they could not sail against it. However, they can do so by sailing in a zig-zag pattern. The sails have to be moved so that they can still catch the wind, and this pushes the hull of the ship along diagonally. Then the sails are moved so that the ship sails along a different diagonal. Sailing like this is called ***tacking****. Old-fashioned, square-rigged ships did not tack easily because the sails had only limited movement. The first sailors to use tacking were from ancient Egypt and East Africa.*

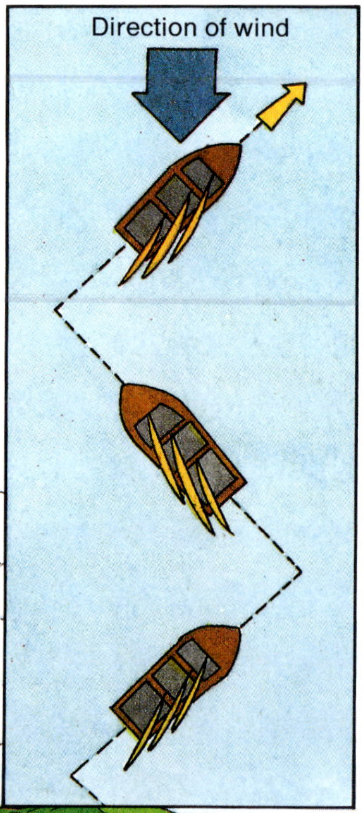

7. Could someone possibly lift the whole world?

In about 250 B.C., the Greek mathematician Archimedes worked out a theory which showed how someone could lift the whole world using a lever. A bar becomes a lever when it is placed on a ***pivot*** *or* ***fulcrum****. When you push down on one end, the other end goes up. You can lift very heavy objects if you use a long lever and put the fulcrum as near as possible to the object you want to lift. To lift the world, you would need a strong lever, millions of kilometres long!*

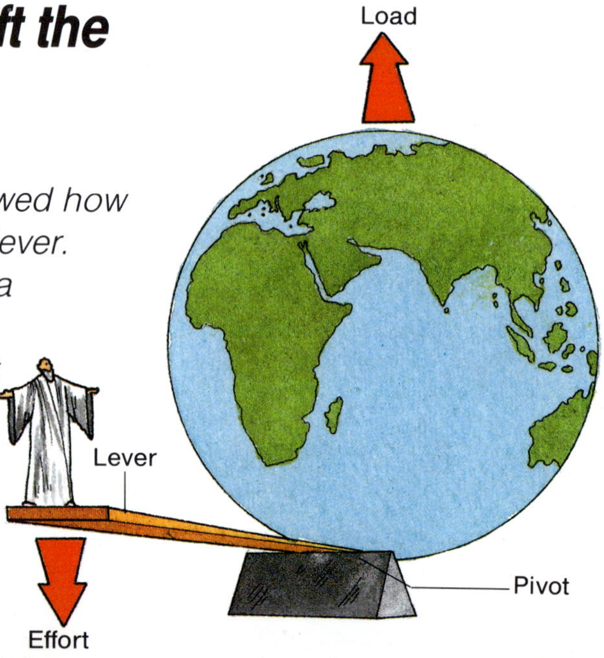

8. Do we still use water wheels?

Water wheels have been used for hundreds of years, often to work flour mills. A large wheel, with paddles on its outside rim, stands in a stream. The force of the water flowing over or under the wheel, pushes against the paddles and turns the wheel. This turns the grindstone inside the mill. There are still a few water-driven flour mills, but today water wheels are mainly used to make electricity. Water from a reservoir flows out through a special kind of water wheel called a ***turbine****. This turns very fast and powers the generator which makes the electricity.*

9. Are there such things as buses without engines?

In some cities, you can see trolley buses – buses without engines which run on electricity supplied by overhead cables. These buses are quiet and clean. Unfortunately, they cannot travel where there are no overhead cables. Trolley buses are no longer widely used in Britain, but you can see them in many other countries in Europe, in Canada and the USSR.

10. Do we really use chips to make a computer work?

*Computers use **silicon chips**. These are tiny pieces of the mineral silicon, with electrical circuits printed on them. They make it possible for the computer to store huge amounts of information.*

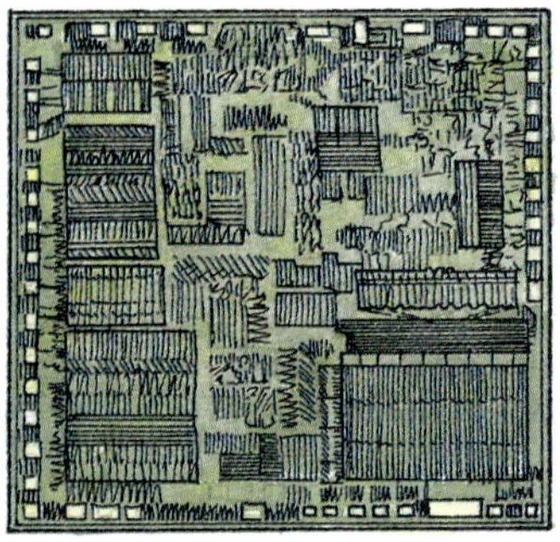

11. Was there once a steam-driven flying machine?

In 1869 a man named Frederick Marriot built a model of an airship, with propellers powered by a steam engine. The model worked indoors in relatively still air, but not outside in the wind.

12. Do wild animals carry radios?

*Scientists often fix radios to wild animals, to help find out where they go and what they do. These are not ordinary radios, but tiny **transmitters** which send out signals. The scientist can pick up the signal on a receiver. For example, a scientist might fix a special collar to a bear. The transmitter is in the collar. It gives out a special signal which is different from that given out by any other bear's transmitter. This means the scientist knows exactly which bear is sending out the signal. It is possible to tell where the bear goes and even to know when it has settled down to sleep. In this way, the scientist can learn a lot about the lives of animals that would otherwise be impossible to track.*

13. How can water travel uphill?

Water can only flow downhill, pulled by the force of gravity. But water in a canal can be made to go uphill. It can do this using ***locks****.*

A lock has two gates that go right across the canal. Each gate has a door called a paddle. When a boat wants to enter the canal, the paddles in Gate A are raised to let the water flow out of the lock. When the water in the lock is at the same level as the boat, Gate A is opened and the boat sails in. Gate A is closed and the paddles lowered. The paddles in Gate B are opened, the lock fills up with water and the boat rises. When the lock is full, Gate B is opened and the boat sails out. Most locks can be operated by hand. Canals that carry large shipping have locks that are opened by engines. In many countries canals were once an important means of transporting goods.

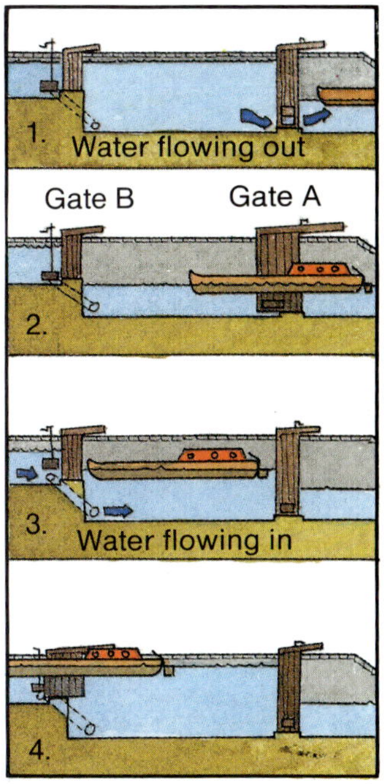

A ship travels through a lock on the Panama Canal, one of the world's busiest canal systems.

14. Did someone really invent a bicycle that was also a shower bath?

This idea dates from 1897. It was called a velocipede shower bath. *The cyclist was supposed to pedal hard. This would work a pump that carried water from a bath beneath the velocipede up to the shower head. The water then soaked the cyclist. The idea did not catch on!*

15. Are there trains that can float above their track?

It is not magic that enables a heavy train to float just above its track, but magnetism. Trains travel faster if they do not actually touch the track as they move, so engineers use the power of magnets to lift them. This is called **magnetic levitation**. *Magnets can attract or repel each other, depending on how they are arranged. One kind of train works using attraction. There is a magnetic guideway beneath the track. Magnetic arms along the base of the train reach under the guideway and are drawn by magnetic force upwards, towards it. This action lifts the train above the track. In another system (shown here), magnets under the train repel the guideway, so lifting the train. In both cases the weight of the train equals the magnetic lift, so the train hovers above the track.*

16. Will we ever be able to fly to Australia in less than two hours?

There are several ideas for very fast aircraft that will fly into orbit 300 kilometres above the Earth. One of these, called HOTOL, could fly from Britain to Australia in less than two hours, taking off and landing at ordinary airports. At first, HOTOL would be automatic, with no pilot or passengers. It would carry satellites into space. Later, there might be a version to carry passengers.

17. Can helicopters fly upside-down?

Helicopters cannot fly upside-down (though a few kinds can loop the loop). A helicopter has rotor blades above it. These spin rapidly, pushing the air downwards and lifting the helicopter up. This means that flying upside-down is impossible, as the blades would be pushing the air upwards and so forcing the helicopter down.

18. Was there really a photographic hat?

In the 1890s, there was a craze for trick cameras, called 'detective cameras'. People hid tiny cameras in all sorts of places: in cravats, in books, in bags and even in their hats. The camera was fixed inside the hat with the lens poking upwards through a hole in the crown. To take a photograph, you had to take off the hat. It must have been hard to use without anyone noticing.

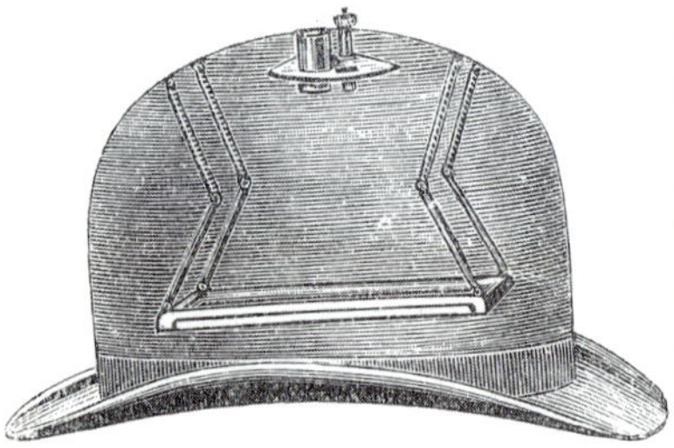

A pig being loaded into a gas pipe.

19. Who would put a pig in a pipe?

The gas board would! A 'pig' is a robotic device that travels through gas pipes with the gas. The metal pig is held against the inner wall by magnetism. Sensors on it can tell if the pipe is damaged. As it checks the pipe, the information the pig collects is stored on a small computer inside it. 'Pig' stands for Pipe Internal Gauge.

20. Are there really aircraft that take off and land on water?

Aircraft that can land, float and take off on water were first built in 1911. They were called **flying boats** *or* **sea-planes** *and were used to great effect by the British in World War 1. Instead of having wheels and landing gear underneath them, like today's aircraft, they were boat-shaped. In 1939, the airline Pan American Airways used a flying boat to run a regular passenger service across the Atlantic. Small flying boats are still used in some places.*

21. Is there rubbish in space?

Yes. There are rockets, old satellites and even tools that astronauts have dropped. There is no gravity to pull them down to Earth. They just stay there, spinning round us in orbit.

22. Has there ever been a machine for rocking a baby's cradle?

This design from the 1870s is for a rocking chair. It rocked a cradle and operated a butter churn at the same time. The inventor thought that a woman could use this chair while she did her sewing. The idea didn't catch on.

23. Can you post a letter through the phone?

*Telephone lines can be used to send letters with a system that is called **facsimile transmission** (or FAX). A FAX machine is linked to your telephone line. The document you want to send is scanned by a photo-electric cell in the FAX machine. This detects the light and dark areas on the document and turns the information into electronic signals. At the other end of the telephone line another FAX machine converts the signals back into light and dark areas and prints out the document. The process takes as little time as a telephone call.*

24. Is it true that the first submarine was built in 1620?

In 1620, a small submarine crossed the River Thames underwater. Its inventor was a Dutchman called Cornelius Drebbel. His craft was made of wood, covered in leather. It was moved by oars and supplied with air through two tubes. These had floats at one end to keep them above the water.

25. Can we get electricity from the Sun?

Energy comes from the Sun in the form of heat. This heat energy can be turned into another kind of energy, electricity, using a ***solar furnace****.*

A solar furnace is made up of mirrors and lenses that catch the Sun's rays and focus (direct) them into a small area. The concentrated heat from all these rays reaches a high enough temperature to boil water. The steam produced can be used to drive a generator that makes electricity.

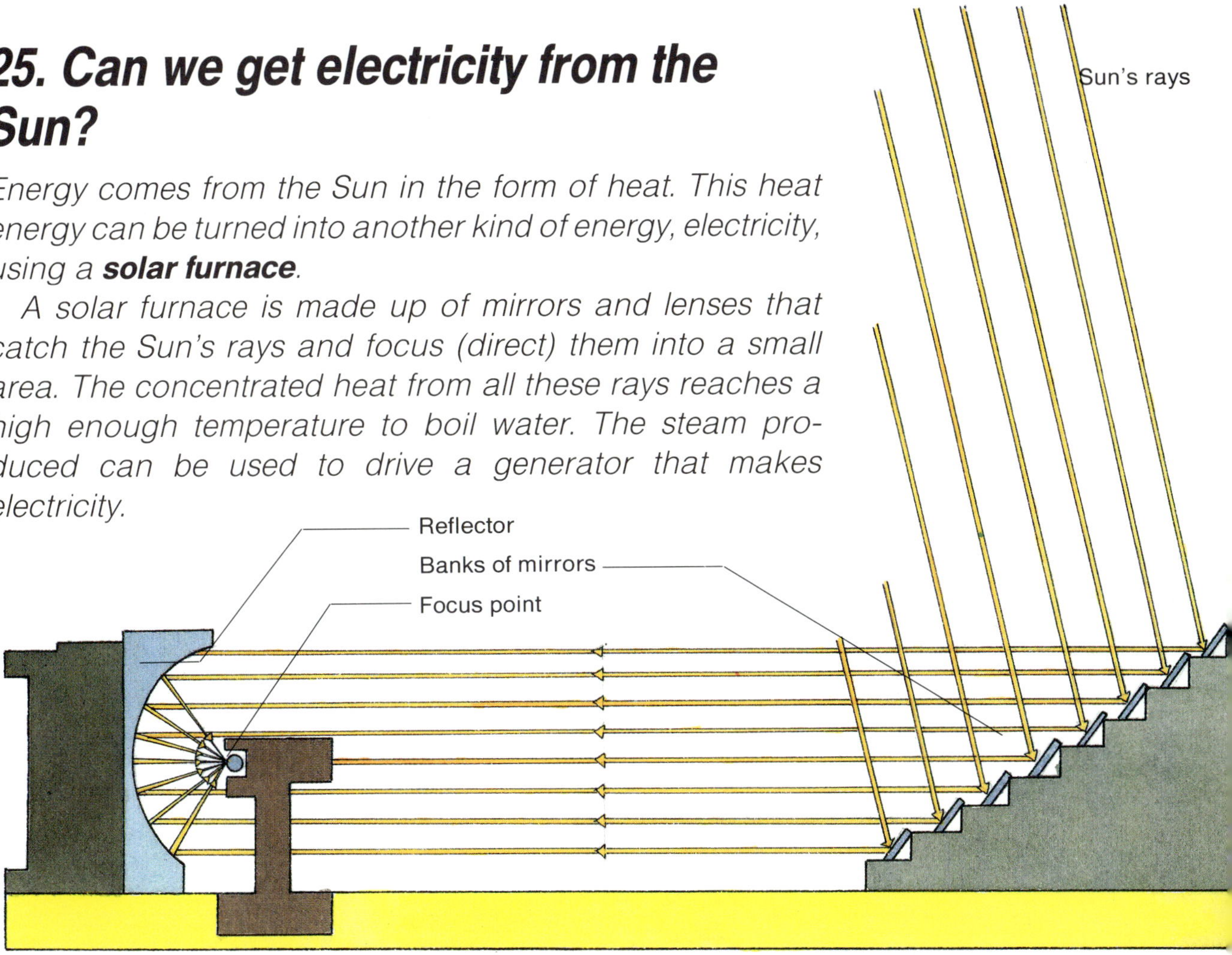

26. Can machines read books?

A computer can be made to 'read' print – or even handwriting – using an ***optical scanner****. A moving beam of light passes over the page. It turns what it 'sees' into information that can be stored in the computer's memory and reproduced in printed form later.*

This computer is being used to scan a printed page which then appears on the screen.

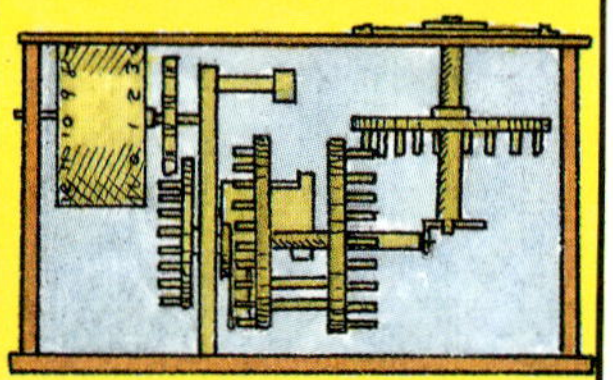

27. Are adding machines a modern invention?

No, adding machines have been around for more than 300 years. The first one was invented in 1645 by a French mathematician called Blaise Pascal. The machine, which used a system of cogwheels, could only add and subtract. There was a special version for adding money. Later, more complicated machines, which could also divide and multiply, were invented. Machines like Pascal's were used for hundreds of years until modern calculators were invented.

28. Are cars actually built by robots?

Robots are used in many factories, especially those where cars are made. The robots can weld, paint and do many other jobs that once had to be done by people. The robots that do these jobs do not look much like people – they are mechanical arms, called ***robotic arms****, which can be programmed by computer to do different kinds of jobs. They are complicated machines which have to be able to move like a human arm – bending, stretching and twisting. They must also be able to judge distances and all this takes a lot of programming.*

Robotic arms are useful in factories where a lot of very boring jobs must be done. A robot can work 16 hours a day, without a break. They are also used to do jobs that people cannot do – such as handling dangerous substances. In the picture opposite, a robot is being used to make a car door.

29. Can you run a car on sugar?

Sugar can be made into a chemical called ethanol. Ethanol is a kind of alcohol that can be used as fuel when mixed with petrol. The ethanol makes the petrol last longer. In countries such as Brazil, where petrol is expensive and where it is easy to grow sugar cane, the mixture is used in ordinary cars.

30. Do boomerangs really come back?

Boomerangs are a kind of throwing-stick that the Aboriginal people of Australia traditionally use for hunting. Most boomerangs are designed simply to hit their target. But some are carved in a special curved shape that makes them travel in a huge circle.

31. Can you wear a television on your wrist?

There is a television that is so small it fits into a wristwatch. The screen is made up of a display which contains liquid crystal cells. The chemicals in the cells are affected by an electrical current flowing through them. As the current changes, the cells become light or dark, so forming the picture. As well as showing your favourite programmes, it also tells the time!

32. Were gas cookers really once made of wood?

Large numbers of gas cookers, made in the 1860s, looked as if they were made of wood. Fortunately, the wood was only on the outside. The inside of the stoves was cast iron, surrounded by a layer of clay. The wood and the clay helped to prevent heat from escaping from the oven. The wood may have made the stoves look attractive, but it can't have made them very safe!

33. Is there such a thing as a flying bedstead?

The 'flying bedstead' was a nickname for an aircraft made by Rolls Royce in the 1950s. People thought it looked like an old-fashioned iron bed. It could take off and land vertically (straight up and down). Modern **VTOL** *(Vertical Take-Off and Landing) aircraft look like ordinary aircraft – but they all developed from the flying bedstead.*

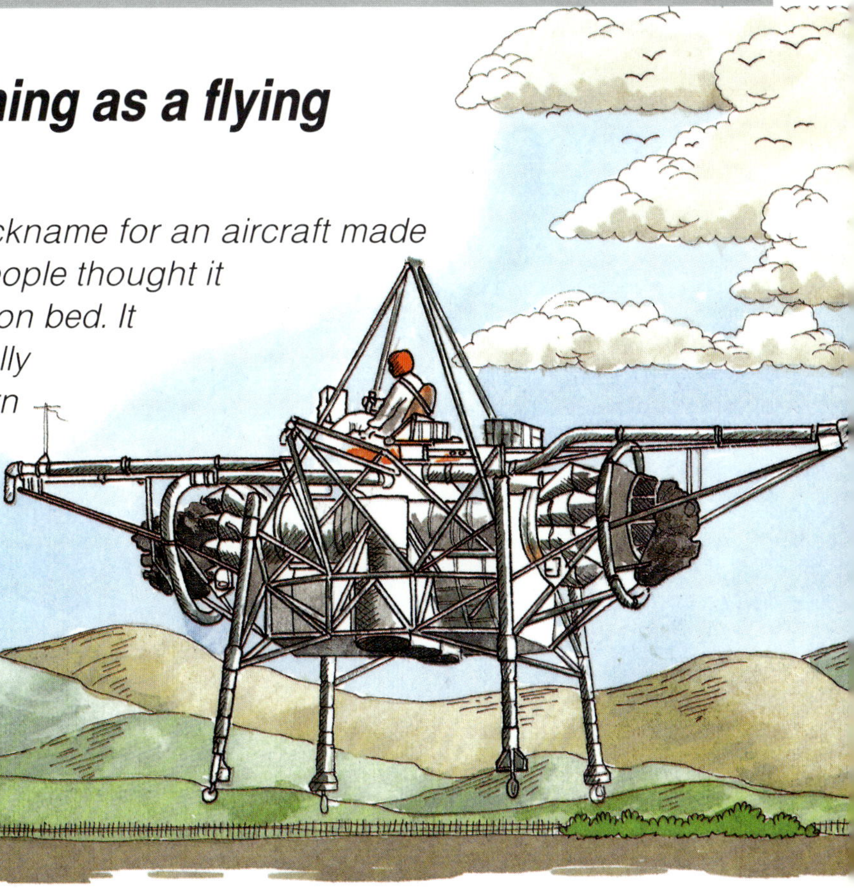

34. Is there really a train that goes at 270 kilometres an hour on ordinary rails?

The fastest train in the world is the French Train a Grande Vitesse *(TGV). It is powered by electricity from overhead cables. It can travel at up to 270 kilometres an hour on ordinary rails that have been modified to carry the train at high speed. The TGV can run on rails that have not been modified – but it cannot go as fast on these.*

35. Can planes fly without a pilot?

In a modern aircraft, the pilot does not have to be in charge of the controls all the time. When the aircraft is cruising, the pilot can use the ***autopilot*** *or* ***automatic pilot****. This is not really a robot, but a system built into the aircraft's controls. This will fly the aircraft at the right height and speed, and in the right direction. The human pilot can regain control at any time.*

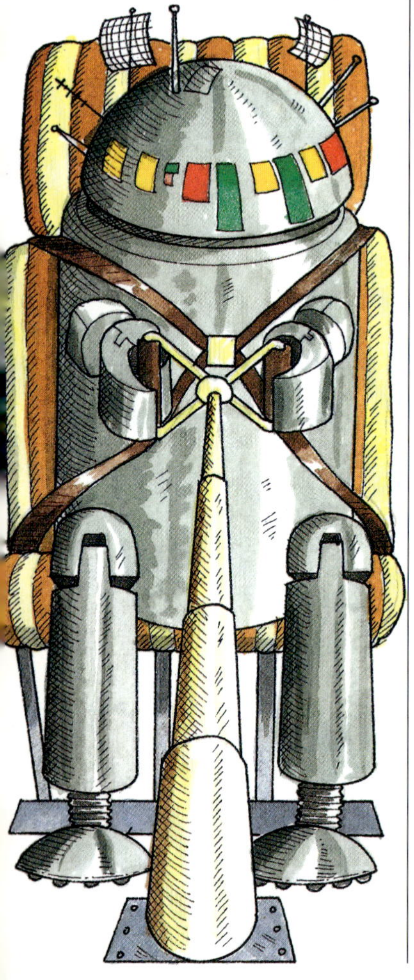

36. How far can a submarine go without surfacing?

There are two kinds of submarine: diesel-electric and nuclear-powered. Diesel-electric submarines have to come to the surface quite often, to recharge the batteries that they use while they are under water. Nuclear-powered submarines do not need to do this, so they can stay under water for a very long time. In 1960, an American submarine, Triton, *sailed under water around the world, a total of 57,946 km. Other nuclear-powered submarines have sailed right under the polar ice pack from Alaska to Greenland.*

37. Can radar help us see in the dark?

Radar (**RAdio Detection And Ranging**) was invented in World War 2, and is used by aircraft and ships to 'see' in the dark. It works by beaming out radio signals. If these meet something solid, they bounce back and are picked up by a receiver. These 'echoes' are displayed as points of light on a screen. The distance and direction of the object can be calculated from the position of the lights.

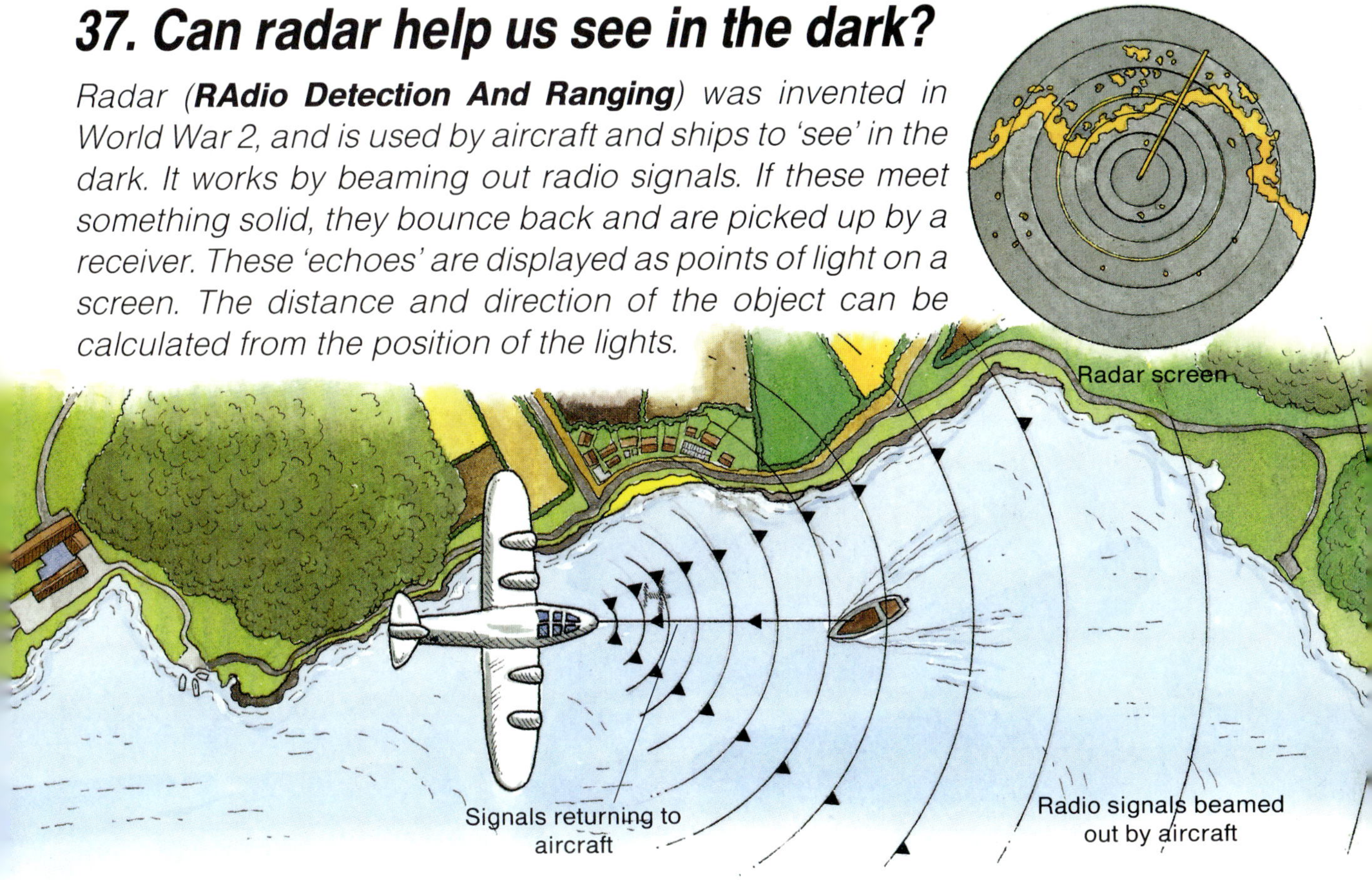

38. Is there really such a thing as an electric lavatory?

Most lavatories use water to get rid of human waste. But this uses up a lot of water and in some places there is not all that much to spare. One solution to this problem is to make a lavatory that burns the waste. The electric lavatory is a bit more complicated to use than a flush lavatory. Before you use it, you have to line the bowl with a piece of wax paper. After you have used it, you step on a lever which takes the waste down into a steel ashpan. Here, the waste is incinerated (burned) until it becomes ash.

39. Can computers talk to us?

Computers can be made to talk using something called a ***voice synthesizer****. The voice you hear is that of a real person. Thousands of words are recorded and turned into electrical signals that can be stored in the computer's memory in digital form. When the computer is activated, the signals are turned back into sounds by the speech synthesizer. It sounds almost the same as human speech.*

40. Do ships and submarines really use sound to find out what is happening under water?

Ships and submarines use a system of sounds called Sonar to find out what is happening under water. Sonar stands for ***SOund Navigation And Ranging****. There is passive Sonar and active Sonar. Passive Sonar just means listening out for the sound of a submarine under the water. With active Sonar, sound waves are beamed out into the water. If the sound waves meet a solid object, such as a wreck, a submarine or ice, they set up an echo. The Sonar system can work out how big the object is and how far away it is. Sonar can also be used to find shoals of fish, and can even show what sort of fish they are.*

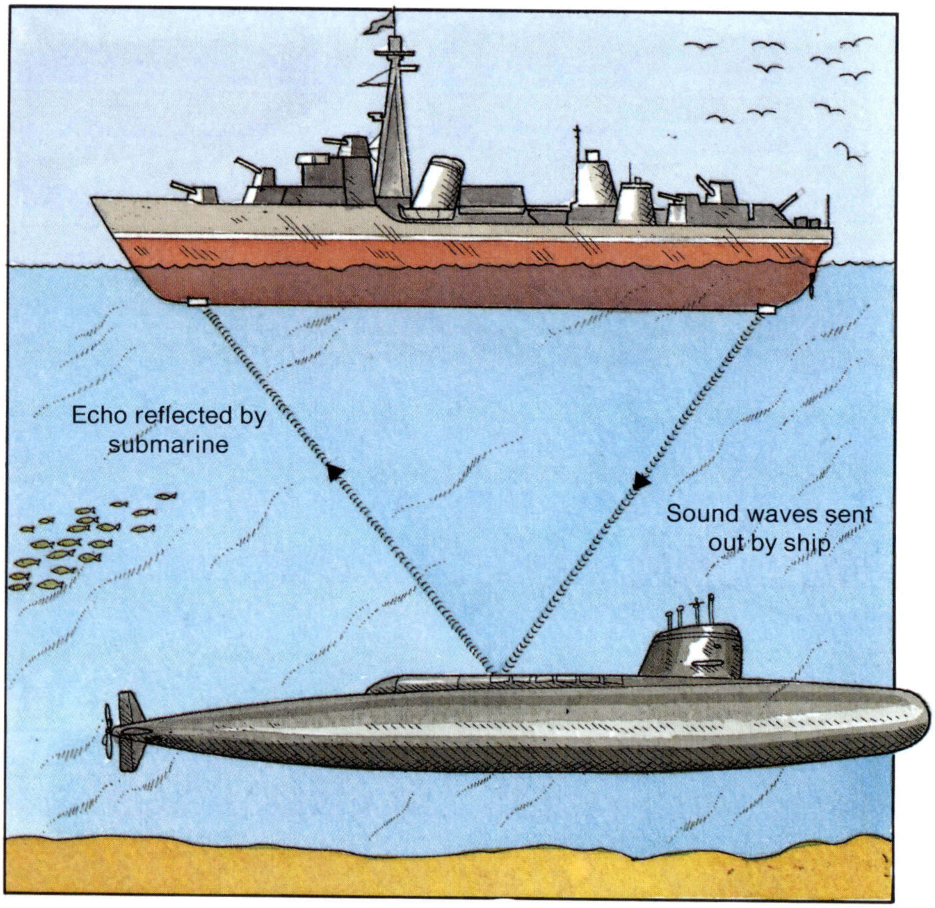

41. Can pianos play themselves?

Pianolas, *or pianos that play themselves, were invented in the 1890s. They look like ordinary pianos, but have machinery inside them that plays the piano keys. The machinery employs a roll of paper with a pattern of holes in it. As the roll moves, air passes through the holes and works valves, which make the keys play.*

A hundred years ago, it was common for people to entertain themselves by singing at home. The pianola *enabled many people to make music without actually being able to play the piano.*

---

42. How deep can a submarine go?

As deep as it is possible to go! A **bathyscaphe** *is a diving vessel designed to explore the ocean depths. In 1960 the bathyscaphe* Trieste *dived 10,916 metres into the Pacific Ocean's Mariana Trench. This is the deepest known part of the world's deepest ocean. The bathyscaphe is made of two parts: a steel cabin where the pilot sits, and a float which is lighter than water. There are tanks on the side of the vessel which, when filled with water, make it sink. To rise again, the pilot releases quantities of iron shot. This lightens the vessel which is then pulled up by its float.*

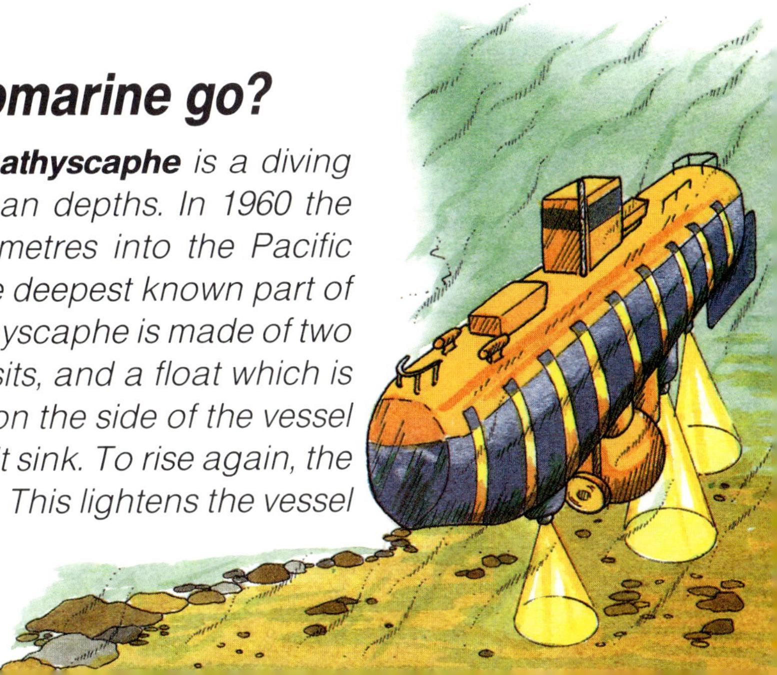

43. Can we really use radar for cooking?

Radar was invented in World War 2 as a way of using high-frequency radio waves to help pilots 'see' in the dark (see page 21). The same sorts of radio waves are used in microwave ovens, where they are beamed through food. These waves make the food's molecules (the tiny particles of which it is formed) move very fast, first in one direction and then in another. As they move they get very hot. The result, of course, is hot food.

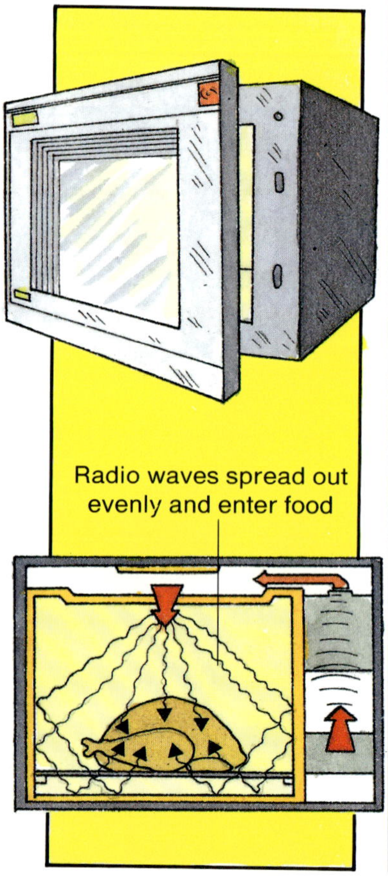

44. Can you ride a bicycle on water?

The Victorians thought up all sorts of strange ideas for gadgets and machines. One of these was an 'aquatic cycle'. This looked similar to an ordinary tricycle, apart from the wheels which kept the cycle afloat and were fitted with fins to help propel it through the water. The 'aquatic cycle' could travel on land as well as on water. Pedalling it must have been hard work, especially in rough weather.

45. Could satellites in space really make electricity on Earth?

A satellite in space could be used to collect energy from the Sun and beam it to Earth. The satellite would have to carry large numbers of ***solar cells****. These are made of tiny slivers of the mineral silicon, painted with special chemicals. When sunlight falls on these cells, it flows across the layer of chemicals on the surface of the cell, and this produces a small amount of electricity. The electricity from all the solar cells on the satellite could be collected, turned into microwaves and beamed to Earth, where they would be turned back into electricity.*

46. Are there flush lavatories on the space shuttle?

Astronauts need lavatories as much as anyone! There are flush lavatories on the space shuttle, but they have been specially designed to overcome the problem of weightlessness. To prevent the waste from floating about in space, the shuttle lavatory has a special system of flushing. There is a vacuum pump which sucks waste away as the lavatory flushes. Liquid waste is carried off into a tank and, after a while, dumped overboard. Solid waste is freeze-dried and brought back to Earth.

CAN YOU BELIEVE IT?

Suppose it is noon (12.00p.m. or 1200 hrs) in London ...

It will be 7a.m. (0700 hrs) in New York ...

4a.m. (0400 hrs) in California ...

The world is divided into ***time zones****. As you travel westwards, the time zones get earlier. As you travel eastwards, they get later.*

47. Why aren't cars made of plastic?

Car bodies are almost always made from metal, since it is a strong and cheap material. Manufacturers have tried using plastic – but it costs too much. A few special cars are made from fibreglass, like the one shown here. Plastic is used mainly on the inside, for the instrument panel, seat covers and steering wheel.

and 10p.m. (2200 hrs) in Sydney, Australia.

48. How can you arrive somewhere before you've left?

You can arrive somewhere earlier than when you set out – if you travel very quickly from one time zone to another. For example, Concorde *can fly from London to New York in just over three hours. In New York, the time is five hours earlier than it is in London. When* Concorde *arrives in New York, it gets there two hours earlier than when it left London!*

49. Do hovercraft really wear skirts?

Hovercraft blow air downwards on to the surface beneath them. The air forms a cushion beneath the hovercraft. This cushion has to be kept in place – if too much air escapes it will not work properly and the hovercraft will not hover. There is a flexible rubber skirt all around the base of the hovercraft, which traps this air cushion. Hovercraft can travel on mud, ice, river rapids and choppy seas.

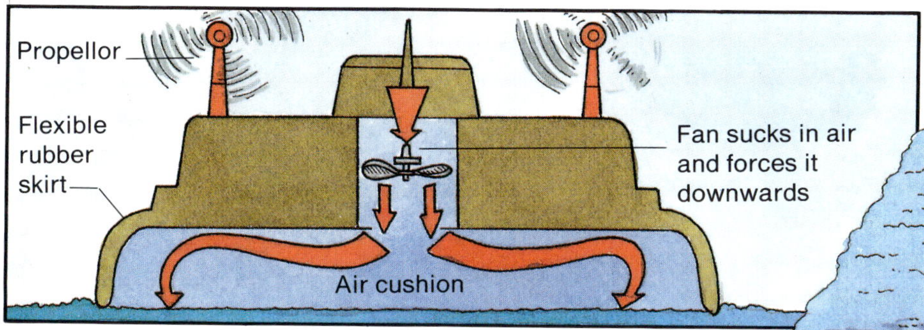

50. Is it possible for a car to travel at over 1,000 kilometres an hour?

Several specially-designed cars have gone faster than 1,000 kilometres an hour. The official record of 1,019.4 kilometres an hour was set in 1983 by a British driver named Richard Noble, in a jet-engined car called Thrust 2. *There is a faster unofficial record – set in 1979 by driver Stan Barret in a rocket-powered car called* Budweiser Rocket. *It reached a speed of 1,190.377 kilometres an hour.*

Thrust 2 *was made of tubular steel and aluminium panels. Its jet-propelled engines used 189 litres of fuel per minute.*

51. Can an aeroplane fly without an engine?

There are many aircraft without engines; they are called gliders. They are very light and designed to float on currents of air. A glider carries only one person. It is pulled into the air by winches on the ground, or by a small aeroplane. Once the glider has achieved a flying speed great enough to overcome the force of gravity, the tow line is released. The glider pilot uses currents of rising air to make the glider float upwards and wind to make it go in the right direction. The furthest a glider has been able to fly is 15,000 kilometres.

The air passing over the wing travels faster than the air passing underneath. This reduces the air pressure over the wing and lifts the glider.

52. Are there robots that can fetch your slippers?

People have often dreamed of making a robot that could do jobs around the house, such as fetching slippers. Many people have tried to do this but it is virtually impossible to programme a computer (that's all a robot is really) to know, for example, where you had left your slippers or even which ones were yours. So, as yet, there are no robots that can fetch slippers and there probably never will be.

53. Are there really machines for voting?

Voting machines are used in America. They were invented in 1892 and looked like the one above. Today's machines show the names of each candidate. The voter moves a pointer to show who he or she is voting for. This works a counter inside the machine which records each vote. The election results can then be quickly gathered.

54. Can a mechanical man play chess?

In the late 1800s, there was a famous 'robot' that played chess. It was a mechanical man, who sat in front of a cabinet as he played. The cabinet had doors in it, and people could look inside. It seemed as if there was no one else there, and that the mechanical man was actually playing. But, in fact, someone was hidden there, moving the chess pieces.

55. Is there really a ship that is made to sink?

There is a kind of ship that is made to be partly sunk. It is called a **Floating Instrument Platform** *(FLIP). It is towed out to sea and then part of it is flooded so that it sinks, leaving the back sticking up above the surface. It forms a platform for scientific research. It does not move much in rough seas.*

56. Can telephone messages travel through space?

Long-distance telephone calls often travel through space. Telephone messages are carried as electrical signals, along cables, from one telephone to another. When these signals have to go a long way, they may be turned into radio waves and travel part of the way in that form. For really long distances, such as from one continent to another, these radio waves may be beamed up into space, to a **communications satellite**. *This relays the message back to a receiver on Earth, where it is turned back into electrical signals and sent along a cable to a telephone exchange.*

57. Will robots ever be able to do the housework?

It would be hard to programme a robot to do some kinds of housework. It could not tell which clothes were dirty – so it could not do the washing. But robot cleaners can clean floors, and can be programmed to go round obstacles.

58. Is it possible for a car to travel on water?

A car can travel on water if it is watertight and fitted with floats. Volkswagens have been adapted to travel on water – but they make better cars than boats!

59. Can you pump water up from underground without a motor?

People have been using pumps without engines for years – they are called ***hydraulic pumps****, and they are used in many parts of the world. The picture shows how one works. When the piston is raised, it makes a vacuum between the two valves. Water is sucked up through the bottom valve to fill this vacuum. When the piston drops, the top valve opens and the water is pushed up through it. Then the piston is raised again, carrying the water upwards.*

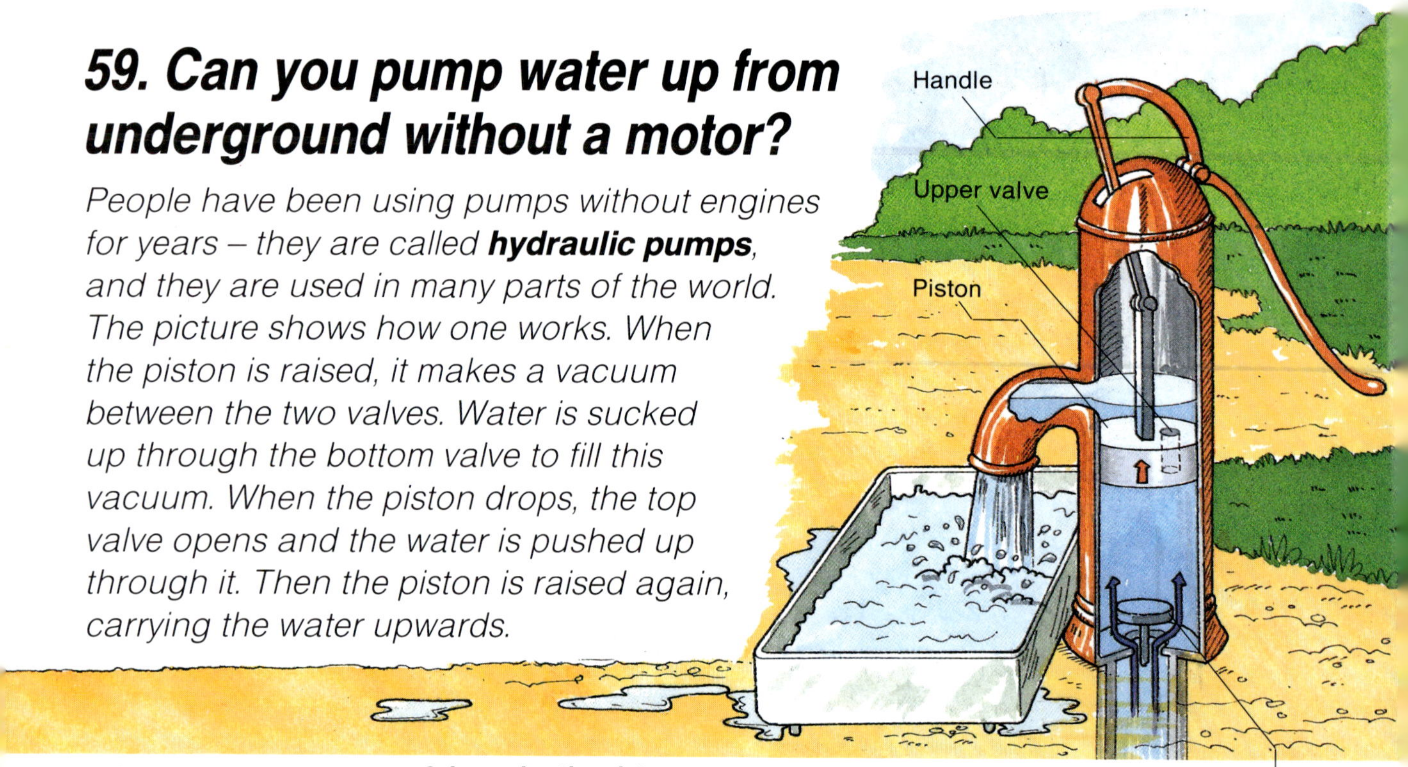

1. Raising the piston. *Water is sucked into the chamber between the piston and the lower valve.*

2. Lowering the piston. *Water is forced up through the top valve.*

3. Raising the piston. *Water is forced out of the pump and more water flows into the chamber.*

---

60. Can we use minerals to tell the time?

Many of the clocks and watches we have today use quartz crystals. This mineral is very common and is found in many different kinds of rock including granite and sandstone. When placed in an electrical circuit, the quartz crystals vibrate at a constant rate every second. In clocks and watches this vibration is used to turn an electric motor which then drives the time display on the clock face.

61. Can you refuel an aircraft in mid-air?

It has been possible for one moving aircraft to put fuel into another since the 1930s. The two aircraft must be flying at exactly the same speed. The aircraft receiving the fuel links up with a pipe that trails behind the tanker aircraft. The idea was first thought up for early passenger aircraft, which could not go far without refuelling. Today, it is used by military aircraft when they fly for very long distances.

62. Can you shear a sheep with a machine?

A robot sheep shearer has been invented. The machine picks up the sheep and holds it as clippers remove the fleece. Electronic sensors make sure the clippers never cut the skin.

63. Is there such a thing as an electric hare?

Electric hares are model hares, used in greyhound racing. The hare is carried round the track on an electric rail and the dogs chase it. They never catch it!

64. Does a hover mower really hover?

A hover mower really does hover. A fan forces air into the empty chamber beneath the mower forming a cushion of air. The air pushes down on the ground and lifts the mower. It "hovers" over the ground making it much easier to push over the grass.

65. Can you use water to run an engine?

Steam engines need water to work – but they need fuel, such as coal, as well. Steam engines are not much used today but in the past they powered factory machinery, railway engines, and even cars. Water is heated to make steam which builds up pressure inside a cylinder. The pressure moves a system of pistons and rods, which are used to make the wheels of the engine move.

66. Did dogs once work in kitchens?

If you had been able to see a castle kitchen in the Middle Ages, you might have seen a dog helping to cook the meat. In those days, meat was roasted over an open fire, on a rod called a ***spit****. The spit had to be turned, to make sure that the meat cooked evenly. Sometimes, the spit was joined to a wheel, inside which a dog was penned. The dog's continuous efforts to escape caused the wheel and the spit to turn. This cruel device was called a* ***treadmill****.*

68. Can you lift things with water?

Liquids can transmit force in all directions at once. The diagram below shows how a ***hydraulic press*** *works. If you push down on the small piston at A the pressure is transmitted evenly throughout the liquid to the heavier piston at B. Piston B will be lifted, but only at a fraction of the distance that A moved.*

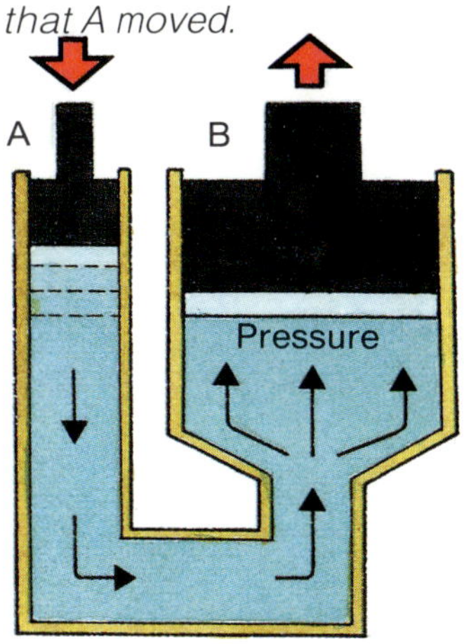

67. Is there a machine that could run forever?

No machine could ever run by itself for ever. However smoothly the parts of a machine move, friction (rubbing) will always slow it down and, in the end, make it stop altogether. Machines need energy – from a person or an engine – to keep them going.

Here is an illustration of one attempt to make a machine that would run by itself forever – a perpetual motion *machine. Like all the others, this too was doomed to failure.*

INDEX